Merry Christmas!
Merry Christmas!
Merry Christmas!

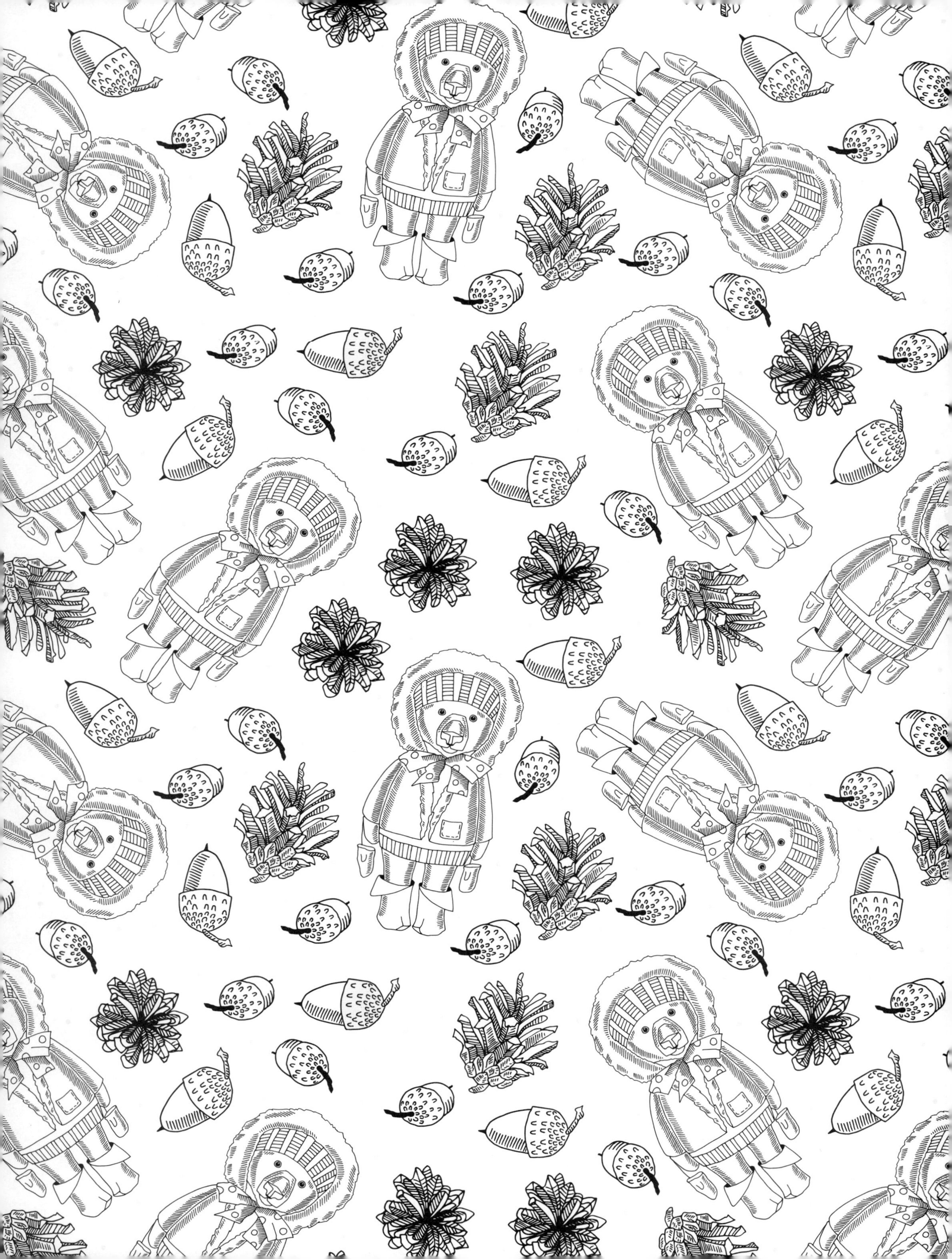

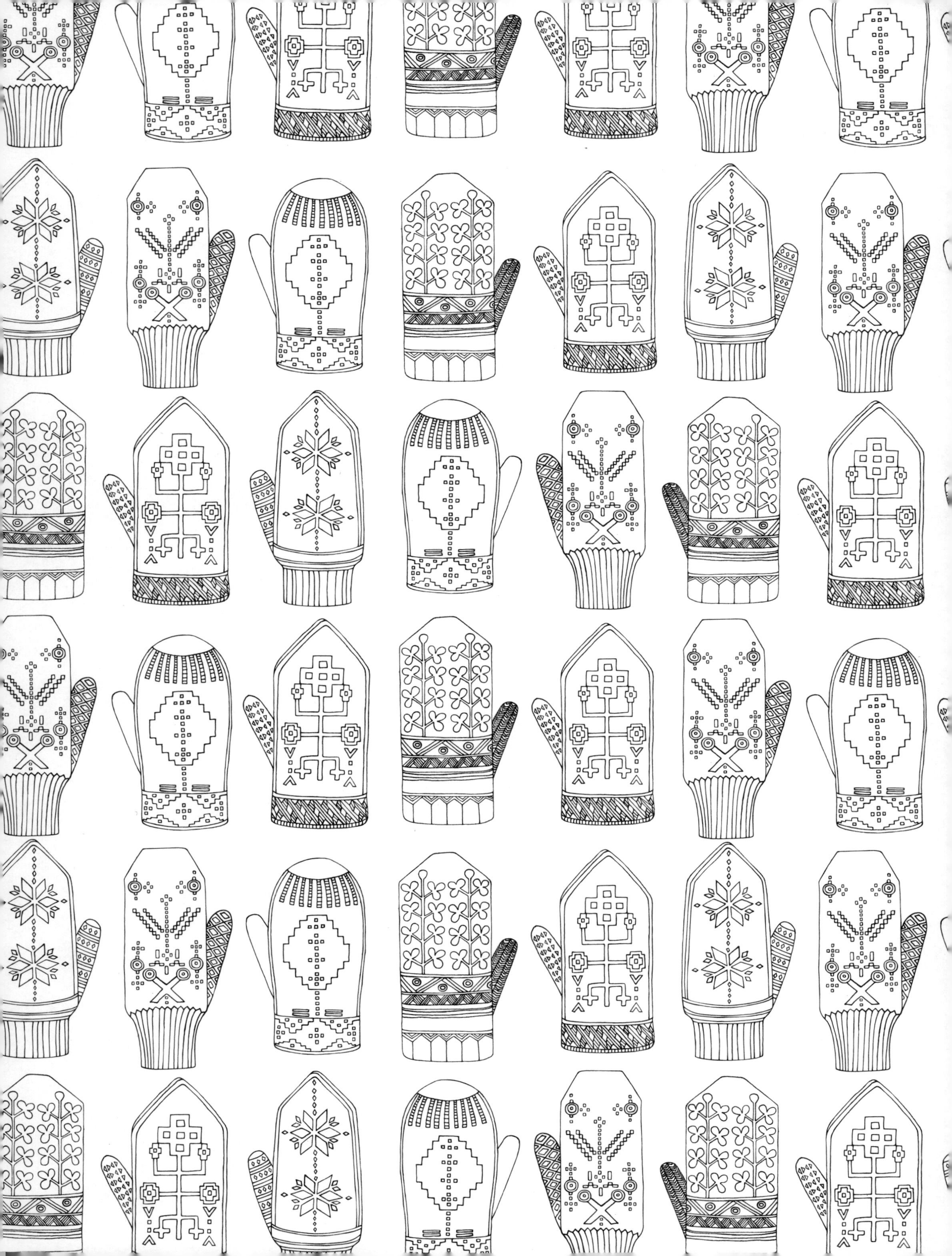

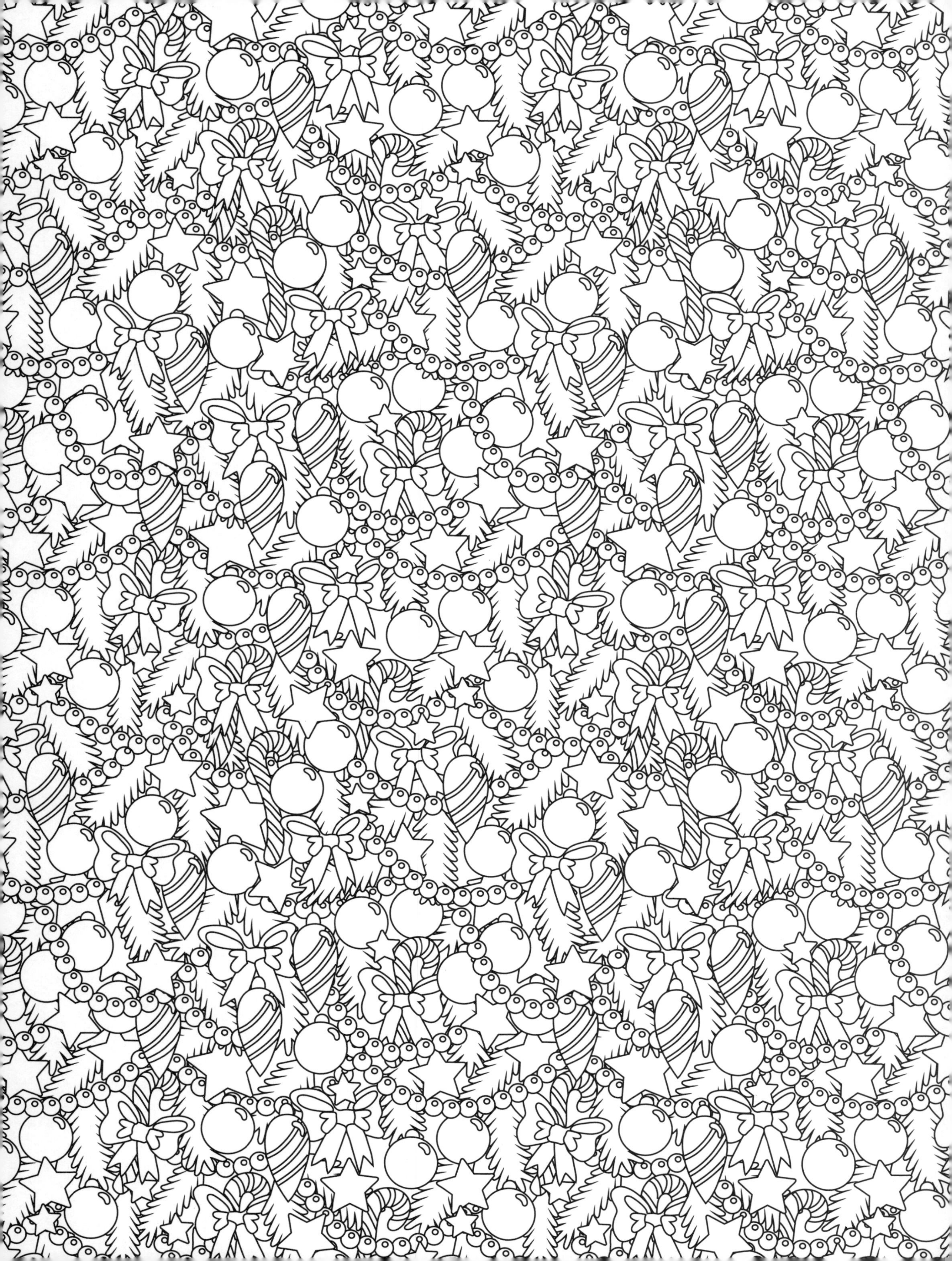

Merry Christmas
2015

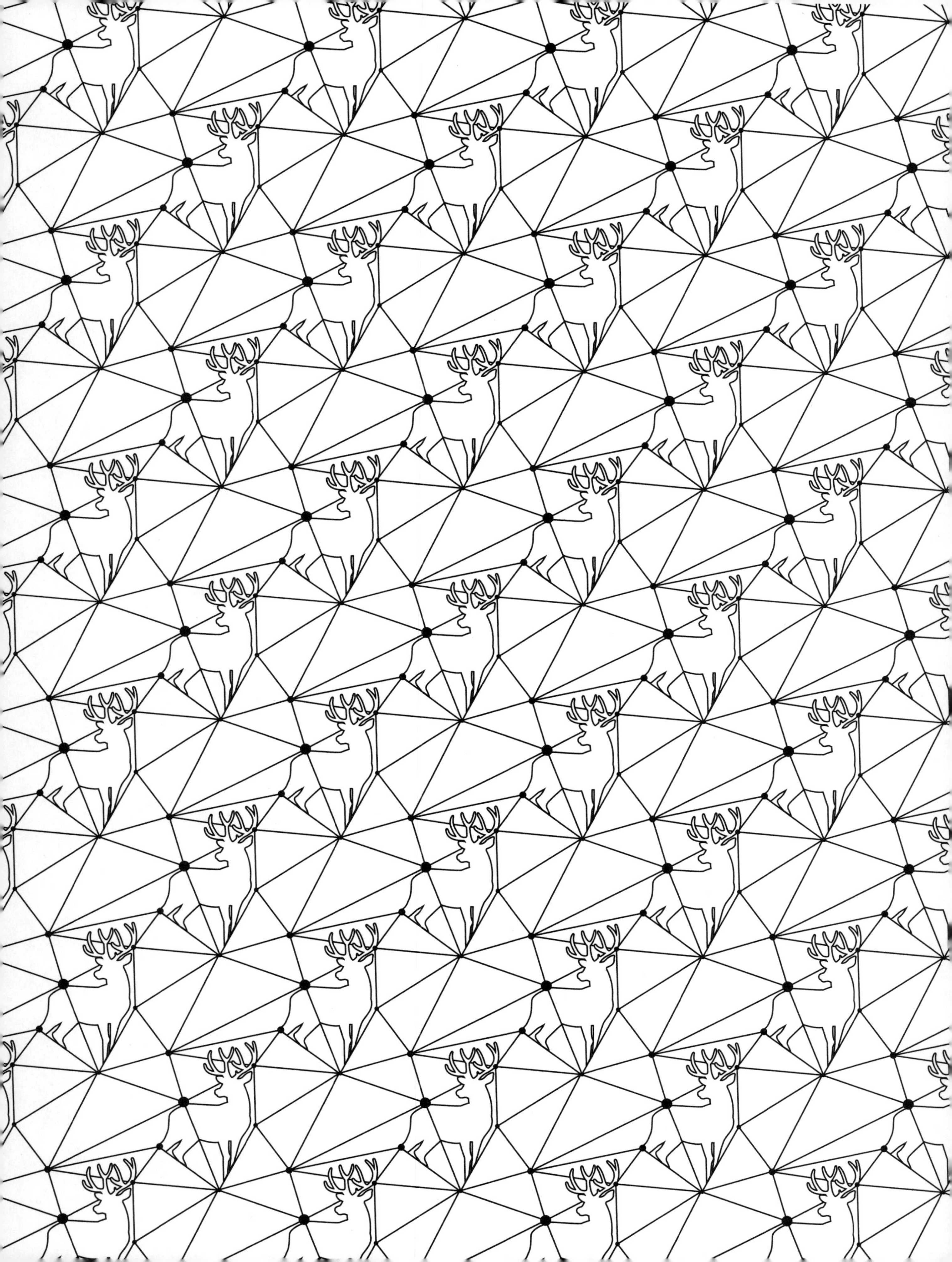

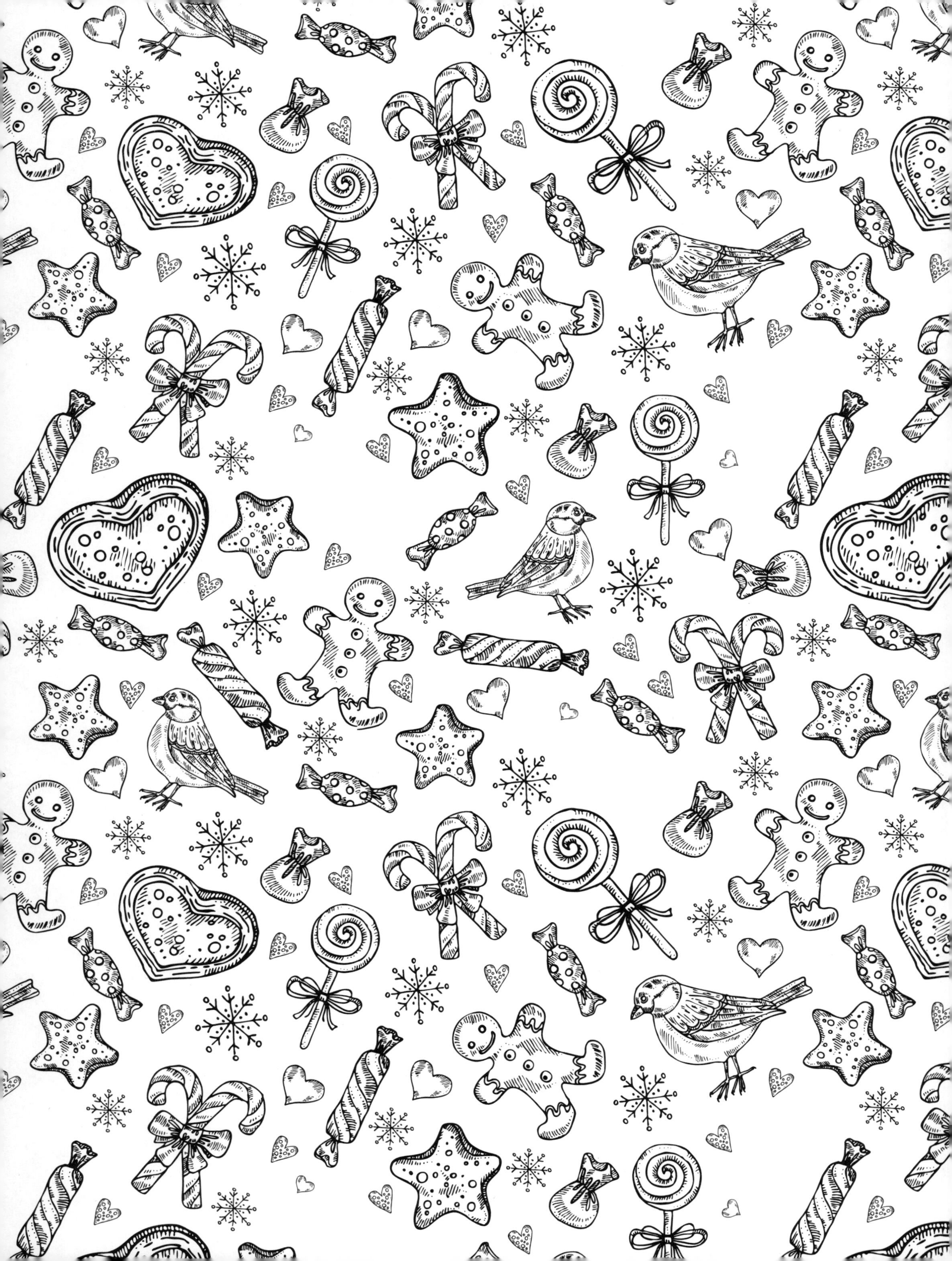

MERRY CHRISTMAS
HAPPY NEW YEAR
WINTER
SNOW
ICE
12

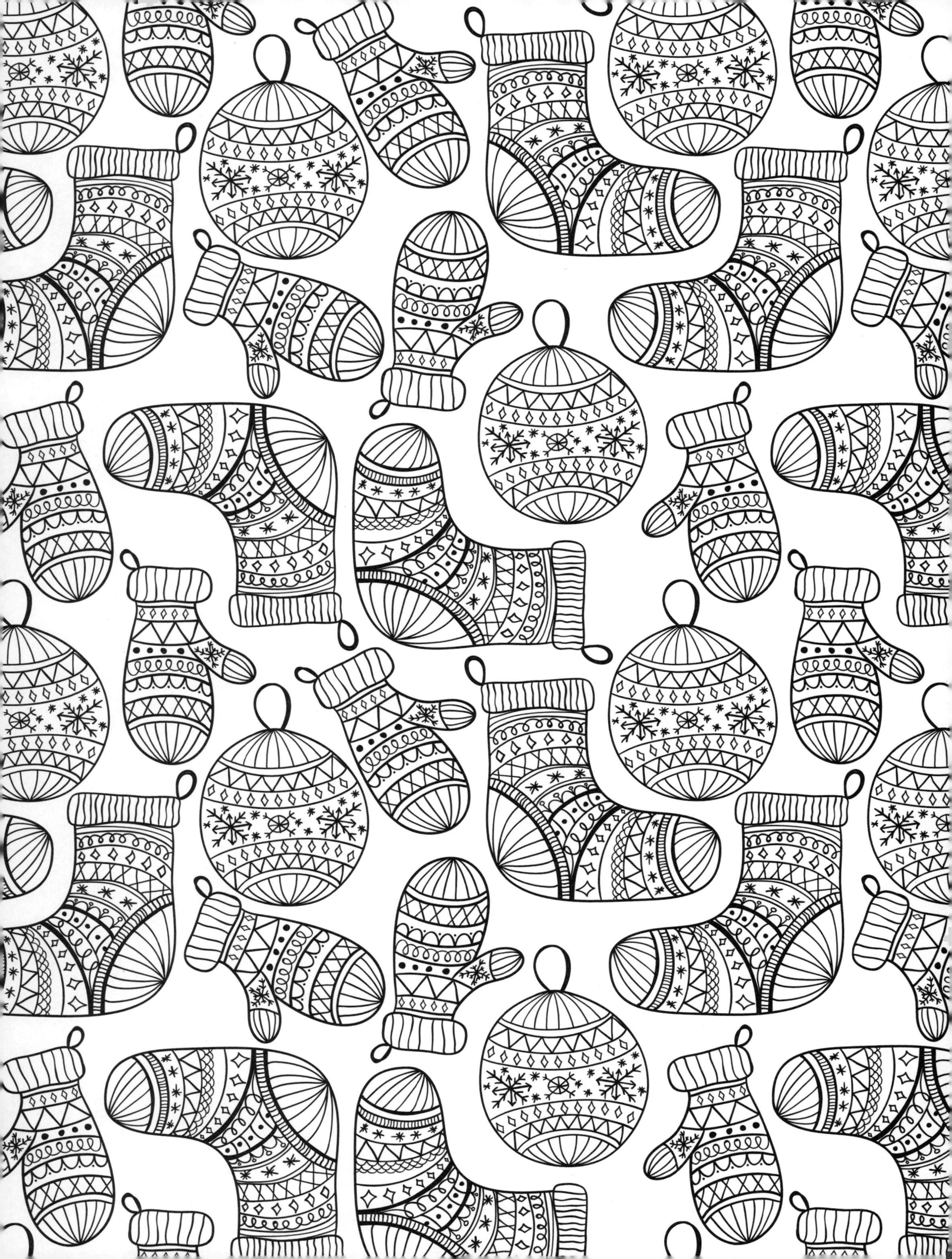